Choosing

To

Dream

By: C. Lynn

Choosing to Dream

HATCHBACK Publishing
Genesee, Michigan 48437

Cover Design by: Superior Interactive

All definitions are taken from Merriam Webster's Collegiate Dictionary.

Unless otherwise indicated all scripture quotations are taken from the New King James Version of the Spirit Filled Life Bible.

ISBN: 978-0-9778155-3-1
0-9778155-3-6

Library of Congress Control Number:
2007922485

Printed in the United States

CONTENTS

DEDICATION

This book is dedicated to all "blocked" dreamers. May you dream again.

ACKNOWLEDGMENT

Thanks to Richard and Crystal for your supportive criticism of my work.

Thanks to my family which allows my dreamer to grow.

Thanks to the Dare to Dream groups from which my creativity receives nourishment.

Thanks to my Creator God, the Dream Giver

INTRODUCTION

The path of dreaming is a spiritual journey. There will be challenges along our path, if not handled properly, will block us from our dreams.

When we choose to dream, we become pioneers. The seemingly invisible road in which we forge is seen by the Dream Giver. He knows our path. Following Him will move us towards our destiny.

My desire is to fan the flame of the dreamer inside of you and to encourage you to be willing to pay the price to live the life in which God has designed. Take courage and make the decision of ***Choosing to Dream.***

Can a Blind Man Dream?

When a man with no sight slumbers, what does he see?
What thoughts parade in his mind while resting?
How can he envision? How can it be?
When he's lacking sight and has no direction
It's comparable to the parable of being a Christian
But not having ever known Christ
Or being a missionary on her mission
But missing her mission of life

Is the darkness increased when he closes his eyes?
Does he depend on his other senses?
Has the lack of dreaming caused our demise
And turned our own kind against us?

For I say yes, the blind can dream
Because dreams embody the mind
Its' only when we come to the point we can't dream
That a man is truly blind

Poet Theodore Files

"To accomplish great things, we must not only act but also dream, not only plan but also believe."

- Anatole France

Why am I Afraid?

"Courage is not the absence of fear but rather the judgment that something else is more important than fear."

- Ambrose Redmoon

"Courage is the resistance to fear, mastery of fear – not the absence of fear."

- Mark Twain

Chapter 1
Facing Fears

An anxious state of mind will paralyze us into inactivity. Firm determination, mental and moral strength will guide us out of the opposition. It takes wisdom, understanding and courage to move beyond our fears.

* Fear of Failure

Just the idea of becoming older and moving toward the future can be a scary thought. When my life is over, what will my family say about me? When my name comes up in discussions of times passed at the dinner table of children I never met, what words will they use to describe me? Answers to those types of questions, help move me beyond the fear of failure.

Believing in my heart every person has a purpose, I began to search within for my own. Connecting to my Creator brought clarity. I knew the types of things I wanted my family to say. I had to take a true inventory of my life which caused some painful "reconstruction."

Stepping out on what I believed would make my life worth living, caused some anxiety. Would I succeed? Do I really have what it takes? Would I be willing to live for what I saw in my heart? By faith, I answered a loud yes to all of those questions.

Now I know if I'd never taken the leap of faith, the question at the dinner table would have been: "Who are you talking about?"

***Fear of Rejection**

I was having a discussion one day with a close friend about rejection. I realized during my childhood, whenever I made a mistake or disappointed my parents, I was rejected. Therefore in order to avoid this terrible feeling, I began to behave in ways to feel accepted. This behavior lasted into my adult years.

Fear of rejection can cause a person not to follow through on a commitment or not follow something that is desired within the heart.

It wasn't until I received the truth of God's word in my heart that I was set free.

Long before He laid down the earth's foundations, He has us in mind, had settled on us as the focus of His love, to be made whole and holy by His love. Long, long ago He decided to adopt us into His family

through Jesus Christ.

Ephesians 1: 4-6
The Message Bible Pg. 2126

Whenever we decide to make a decision to "think outside of the box," the voice of rejection begins to speak. Resistance comes from within as well as without which becomes a stumbling block if not stopped by the truth of the Word of God. I am already accepted. Long before I made any decisions or had taken any action I was accepted in the Beloved.

***Fear of Success**

It takes courage to stay honest with oneself. Sometimes we may be doing well, sometimes too well and we consciously or unconsciously set up ways to self-sabotage our own efforts. Self- sabotage comes from a fear of being successful. One of the greatest friends of self-sabotage is procrastination.

When I find myself experiencing this, I began to listen to what I'm saying on the inside. This is what I usually hear:

Who do you think you are?
Do you really think you deserve this?
What makes you think you're worth it?
How do you know you can do it?

Procrastination is a fear of moving forward. It is a fear of starting something new or different. The cure for fear is love. Be nice to yourself. Give yourself permission to start small and take little steps.

In order to defeat this fear, we must immediately move into action. Buy the business cards, start writing, make a phone call, build the website, start painting, sign up for the dance class, plan the vacation. Forging ahead will begin to cripple the negative voices.

Looking toward the future with hope and clarity demands we overcome the fears of failure, rejection and success.

I choose to be an overcomer.

Let’s Start

“For what is faith, unless it is to believe what you do not see.”

- St. Augustine

Chapter 2
Committed to Becoming

Knowing there is no arrival to who we are allows us the liberty to change. I am excited about this because I don’t have to stay the same. If I liked cabbage last week and I seem to not care for it this week, then it’s okay. Change is an inevitable part of life. Learning to flow with it brings peace. As I keep growing older from year to year, I pray wisdom and understanding will increase.

If you find yourself doing something you thought would bring you to a certain place but in reality it takes you in the opposite direction, it is okay to stop that particular activity. Some people may say that sounds like quitting but let me further explain.

There was a time when I was bothered by my sciatica, so I decided to walk in the shopping mall. This activity was good for my heart also. My husband as well as a few of my friends were impressed by my commitment to an exercise program. All was going well until I ran into one problem, walking was causing my heels to hurt. I had to stop walking. What I decided to do took me in the opposite direction of where I wanted to go. Instead of improving my health, I began hurting myself in another area. I did have a chance to meet some wonderful people whom I saw on a regular basis. (Swimming and getting in the hot tub has proved to be the answer).

Here's another example. Imagine that I was leaving Michigan on my way to the state of Maryland, I would travel east. While on the highway, I see road signs which tell me how many miles I need to travel before entering the state of Colorado. I'm not traveling east at all, in reality I was traveling west. There would be no way of getting to Maryland in the direction I was going. I would now have to stop and turn around but oh, what sights I would have seen!

The same principle can be used in life. When a person is committed to becoming, not to the destination, then every turn in life, whether left, right, heading straight or turning in circles would all play a part. The joy is not always in the results but instead it's in the process of the journey.

I choose to enjoy the ride.

Lighten Up!

"Anyone who has never made a mistake has never tried anything new."

- Albert Einstein

"Humor is the harmony of the heart."

- Douglas Jerrold

Chapter 3
Learning Not to Be too Hard on Myself

Learning not to be our own worst critic takes practice. No, everything we do is not perfect or complete. Neither are our most awful mistakes our conclusions.

*Learning to Like Who I Am

Over the years, I had to learn to like myself. I had to stop comparing myself to others (especially women). No, my hair was not as long. My legs were not as big. I felt my feet were too big for my body. I could go on and on comparing myself with others and always coming up with a list of "…..and this is what's wrong with me."

I began to learn to speak positively of myself; looking at the good qualities in which I possessed. This is a learning tool which I practice fiercely: I don't speak negatively of myself (out loud or inwardly) and I do not allow others to do it either. Using this method has helped me to set healthy emotional boundaries. Also believing what the word of God says about me, stops the negative self-talk.

I will praise You, for I am fearfully and wonderfully made; Marvelous are Your works, and that my soul knows very well.
Psalms 139:14

Either I was going to believe the "lies" which had been spoken over my life by others and myself or I was going to believe the truth. If His thoughts of me are of good and not of evil, then why shouldn't I have the same thoughts?

I had to train and condition myself, until it was not a part of my vocabulary anymore that something was wrong with me.

***Learning to Laugh at My Mistakes**

The reality is we as human beings sometimes have inadequate knowledge and faulty judgment. This leads to blunders in choices, taking wrong actions or making wrong statements.

When I find myself in an outcome of one my many errors, if I've hurt someone I apologize. I am going to make mistakes, not excuses but mistakes. It doesn't mean I am a failure or that I'm stupid.

When I was growing up, I was afraid to make mistakes, therefore I made excuses and blamed other people. Being afraid to make a mistake causes a person to lack taking responsibility for ones' own actions.

Now with a healthy view of who I am, I can laugh when I mess up. It didn't cause the world to end and if I really think about it, in 50 years what will it matter!

I choose to laugh at myself.

Let's Pack and Move

"How calmly may we commit ourselves to the hands of Him who bears up the world."

- Jean Paul Richter

Chapter 4
Moving Beyond Insecurity into Self-Confidence

Without reluctance, we must choose to proceed toward the direction of confidence. Faith to believe is the key which unlocks the door.

***Knowing Who I Am is What God Intended**

Insecurity hems us in by fear and anxiety. It makes a person feel not adequately guarded, shaky or unstable.

Distinguishing "which" voice I was listening to played a great part in increasing my self-esteem. I had to accept the following truth into my heart:

...the Spirit of Him who raised Jesus from the dead dwells in you...Romans 8:1a

...for in Him we live and move and have our being...Acts 17:28a

This truth is not based on what I or others may say.

I had to learn to motivate, believe in and have confidence in myself. Mediating on the words of God keeps a guard on my heart and my mind.

***Being Okay with My Strengths and Weaknesses**

Some days I will display my strengths, on other days I will display my weaknesses. If I don't make a big deal out of either, I learn to be okay with myself. I am learning to go much further in life because I've moved beyond my insecurities into my God-confidence.

Having my confidence in God, whether the results are good or bad, moves me toward a greater degree of what He has intended for me.

Because He is my Creator, all of my strengths and weaknesses belong to Him. He alone knows my design and how much pressure it takes to mold, shape and make me.

I choose to trust in His work rather than my own.

Don't Touch the Stove

"Loving me is the second best decision I've ever made, deciding to receive God's love was the first."

- C. Lynn

"The man who moves a mountain begins by carrying away small stones."

- Chinese Proverb

Chapter 5
Living Without Self-Prescribed Pain

We must learn to choose daily to conduct our lives in a manner which will not cause us emotional or mental distress.

***Discontinuing Destructive Behaviors**

Whenever things didn't quite go like I thought they should, I had a set of destructive behaviors from which I would choose. When I hurt, either I hurt others or hurt myself. Some of the negative responses could range from not eating properly, over eating, over spending, watching too much television, having a nasty attitude and the list goes on. I discovered all of this was based on self-hatred. I know that term may sound strong but why would anyone choose to hurt themselves?

When I experienced God's love to a greater degree, I could no longer make sense of these choices. I began to love myself and pay attention to how I felt. When I did this, I began to make better decisions on how I reacted in any given situation.

***Letting Go of Past Hurts and Failures**

When we keep regrets going and rehashing them over and over, the result is our emotions become stunted. Whether it is said out loud or just repeated in our minds, the outcome is the same.

I had to make a choice to forgive either myself or others and move forward. I am not saying this process is quick or easy but it is a necessary process.

***Letting Go of Toxic People**

I chose to use my own definition for toxic people. It is as follows:

Toxic people – a person or persons whose behavior is destructive or harmful to another person; someone who habitually injuries another person; a person whose behavior hinders the activity of another

With that being said, it is clear as to why letting go of toxic people, whoever they may be, is a good, healthy and positive choice.

*** Realizing What Others Think Really Doesn't Matter**

This one proved to be harder in my life because of all the negative messages I received as a child.

These are a few examples:
You're too little.
You're too skinny.
Your head is too big.
You're "four-eyed" (I wore glasses)
You're a really "black" child. (my dark complexion)
You're not smart enough.
You're not pretty enough.

Because of the negative conditioning, I put a lot of work into trying to be "right enough" or "good enough" to measure up to others' expectations.

I began to trust in the Spirit of God which lives on the inside of me but yet being free from the opinions of others proved to be a painful and warring undertaking. I had to release myself from unhealthy relationships and situations which caused me to think less of myself. What I thought of myself proved to be what others thought of me. I began to speak positive words over myself, not just saying them but allowing it to penetrate in my heart and into my belief system.

When the change began to happen, I heard remarks like these:
You sure are becoming prideful.
You think you don't make mistakes.
Please, tell me, what are your weaknesses?

I began to understand I was getting healthy and it made others uncomfortable. When I got rid of my own negative belief systems, I had to take a firm stand against other peoples' negative belief systems about me. I had to become willing to not allow people in their limited thinking to limit me in my own thinking.

I've recently taken the position which includes letting go of a persons' good opinion of me. If I stay there too long, I can be "boxed into" what they think I do best.

It was a tough road but I have my confidence and hope firmly based in God. When I can keep my focus there, what others think *really* doesn't matter.

Is God okay with me? Is my life pleasing to Him? That's what *really* matters!

I choose to love myself.

"When all else is loss, the future still remains."
- Christian Nestell Bovee

Chapter 6
Accepting Losses as a Part of Life

Sometimes when we take a stand for what we believe, people will turn and walk away. It is a part of living and dreaming. When I began to dream and set my life on a course to follow it, I didn't fit in some of the same circles anymore. It was not a good thing nor a bad thing. It was just "one of those things."

In order to gain, there will be some losses. Maybe it will be a loss of a relationship, a position, a group of people or the loss of a certain comfort. Sometimes the revelation of a dream will cause us to come out of denial (which is a loss of a certain reality) and take us into our true reality.

Not being asked to hold a position on the committee, not receiving a role in a play in which you auditioned, not receiving the promotion, being turned down for a job in which you applied…all of these are losses. Not mourning a disappointment can become a wall which separates us from our future dreams.

Losses are a part of life, whether it is good or bad. The point is in order to dream, we have to be willing to face the losses, call them for what they are and have the ability to keep moving forward.

Dreaming demands us to be willing to leave one place and go to the next.

I choose to be willing to move.

What's Cooking?

"Responsibility is the thing people dread most of all. Yet it is the one thing in the world that develops us, gives us manhood or womanhood fiber."

- Frank Crane

Chapter 7
Nourishing and Nurturing Me

With my life rapidly moving toward half of a century here on earth, I had to take a long hard look at how I was treating myself. My hearts' desire is to live until I am 102 years of age. We change from one year to the next but I believe I can do something to help my body make these adjustments more graciously.

Whenever I am out, I pay close attention to elderly people and I honor them all. But there is one type I most admire and they are the ones I have chosen to mimic my life after. They are the ones who grow old gracefully. They are the ones who are full of wisdom. They don't constantly talk of their aches and pains. They understand while they yet have breath, they are to pour out their life experiences to anyone who will listen. They live healthy lives. They have healthy attitudes. They are a joy to be around!

Let's look at two definitions:

1. Nourish – to promote the growth of; to maintain, to support
2. Nurture – to further the development of

God has wonderfully made us into complex beings with many different parts making up the whole. I want to look at a few areas which I decided needed some immediate attention to equip me to achieve the dream which is in my heart.

*** My Health**

One of the areas I needed to immediately take charge of was my health. After some years, I let wisdom decide what was good for me and what activities were no longer healthy for my body. I had to make adjustments based on my body type and family history. I was diagnosed with high blood pressure in my mid-thirties. I took it as a family condition. My mother and father both had it and I knew my own weakness for the taste of salt. The doctor told me some things which I could do to protect my heart and my health but I didn't listen.

Now I hear wisdom. I choose to work out three times per week. I do nothing strenuous or too heavy because I know what my body can handle. I am not trying to lose weight or build muscle mass. My focus is a healthy heart. Since every person is different, we have to do what will build health for us personally.

***My Emotions & My Mind**

I became physically aware I had to nourish and nurture myself emotionally. I had to immediately learn to set healthy boundaries. There was a period in my life where I would experience eye twitching and heaviness in my chest. I noticed it happened more times when I was overly stressed about a situation. I even went to the hospital once and had an overnight stay. They thoroughly checked me for any heart problems, which by the grace of God, it showed everything was normal and healthy. Wisdom began to cry out for me to take a look at my life. Who or what had I allowed in my life to stress me to that level? Now just living I understand I will have certain amounts of stress from time to time but that is not what I am referring to here. This was a huge amount of stress daily. I began to search and pay attention to what was going on when these symptoms began to arise. When I noticed the pattern, I made some ***major*** adjustments.

I had to get certain people out of my life. Those who were long on drama and never coming to a solution for their problems, GONE! Whatever I found myself in that didn't produce emotional health for me, I changed my surroundings. Some of these changes were drastic but they were necessary. I can now say these attacks are far and very few.

I had to become adamantly aware of what I allowed my ears to hear and my eyes to see.

I will set nothing wicked before my eyes.

Psalms 101: 3

Protecting my gates (my eyes and ears) is a daily practice. It helps me to stay focused on the dream which God has given rather than wondering on things to the contrary.

Times of solitude are the most precious commodity. It allows my mind to rest. No work, no play just rest.

***My Soul**

One of the things I despise most is being angry at myself. What causes my soul to anguish in this way is not staying committed to what I said I would do. It causes me great frustration. I am not talking about being inflexible and so constrained that a change in schedule throws me into a tizzy. I'm referring to times when I say "yes" too often. Therefore, the simple word "no" has become a great companion. I've learned from the great Zig Ziglar, if I have to make a decision right away, the answer is no.

I allow myself time to think before I add anything to my schedule. My priorities are God first, then my family. *Everything* else follows!

***My Spirituality**

My personal walk with God is the number one area which I must keep nurtured and nourished. Growing in my relationship with Him is as necessary as food is for my body or air to breathe.

Knowing myself, I have to be on the look out for distractions which try to move in between me and my Christian walk.

Daily I arise and make a choice to allow Christ to sit on the throne of my heart. He rules and reigns so my life can produce the good works He already has prepared for me.

I choose to take care of myself.

Keep it Simple

"Simplicity is making the journey of this life with just baggage enough."

- Charles Warner

Chapter 8
Cherishing Simplicity

Cultivating affection for our basic essentials will help clarify our lives. A man towering 8 feet will not find comfort in a 6 foot bed. Therefore, everyone must choose what simplicity is for themselves.

***In My Material Possessions**

My closet was overflowing with purses. Some were handbags which had been out of style for years. I told myself I just like purses. I still do. But I made a decision not to like them as much.

I function at a higher level when I keep things simple. I don't need a lot of clothes, shoes, etc. I get rid of them if I haven't worn them in a year. I give it away because it eliminates the clutter. My mind is clearer and sharper when I don't have the hassle of taking care of so many "things." I decided I no longer had to "keep up appearances." It drained me of my precious energy and it was hard work.

***In My Relationships**

Because of my upbringing, I thought relationships should be chaotic. I was one of those people who loved the drama of the storm. I had a need to be needed and I was the "fix it" person. I would try to fix your problem whether you asked me to or not.

Now I cherish the simplicity in my relationships. I have experienced to a greater degree the grace of God in my life and now I am capable of showing others grace for their lives. I no longer have to spot out everything I believe is wrong in a persons' life and try to correct it for their good so I can feel better about myself.

We are all on a spiritual journey. We don't all look, talk, dress or act alike. We don't all share the same beliefs about God, politics or child rearing. Yet there is something special about each one of us. God knew exactly what He was doing when He created the world and everything in it. I've learned to like it His way.

I choose to be content.

"By being yourself, you put something wonderful in the world that was not there before."

- George Elliott

"It takes courage to grow up and become who you really are."

- E. E. Cummings

Chapter 9
The Joy of Being Me

All of my life has been a wonderful learning experience including my mistakes, my good times, my failures and my successes. It is all okay. My total life rests in the hands of God and so do the results. I no longer have to be phony or fake. I no longer need to impress anyone. I don't have to try to be perfect. I understand whatever God has for me is for me and there is nothing anyone can do about it. Everyday when I rise, I make a decision to glorify God and be my "best self." What joy and freedom there is in Jesus Christ! What peace there is in knowing Him! What a wonderful revelation to understand that while I was yet a sinner, Christ died for me. Why now do I have to do and be all of these things to feel okay? He loves me just like I am.

I have chosen to live each day with no regrets. I do the best I can do at what I am doing everyday. When I lay my head on my pillow at night, I rest in peace knowing I probably made some mistakes but tomorrow is already full of grace and brand new mercy. I choose to carry no guilt or condemnation.

I went through a process of finding out from my Creator who He designed me to be. I no longer participate in other peoples' ideas for me. So yes, there was a BIG change to the glory of God! Some changes were made abruptly, others are still in the process. There is a price to pay to follow the Dream Giver. I am committed to see it through until the end.

I choose to be only me.

What's Good for Me

"The Heavens are as deep as our aspirations are high."

- Henry David Thoreau

Chapter 10
Living Up to My Own Expectations

While lying in bed early one morning, I allowed my mind to wonder and dream of what I really wanted out of my life. What were the things I wanted to see in my lifetime? I believe it was Gandhi who said, " If you want to see something done in the earth that you do not see, you do it."

There were some things I wanted to see done in my community I had yet to see. I had to make up my mind. By the grace of God, I was going to deposit them into the community. There were some things in my family I had never seen done. By God's grace, I was going to be the one to do it.

I had to believe what I saw and start living up to my own expectations. It is so easy to talk about how bad something is or what other people are not doing. I don't want to be the person that merely talks about the problem. I want to be part of the solution. I had to follow the dream.

Whenever we decide to step forward, especially if we are going to pioneer, there will be resistance. I strongly believe if God placed it in my heart, then He is going to give me all the provision and everything necessary to make it come to pass.

Building strength and endurance for the fight ahead is necessary. Maintaining focus is imperative. There will be plenty of reasons not to move forward and obstacles are inevitable. Being able to discern who and what distractions are is another key principal.

I've found daily, consistent, fervent prayer and time in mediation to be the answer. Knowing God sees, knows, cares and is willing to do something about it takes the pressure off. He gives abundant grace for the journey.

I choose to do what it takes.

Pour It All Out

"Give what you have to someone, it may be better than you dare to think."

- Henry Longfellow

"… die empty."

- Myles Munroe

Chapter 11
Time to Give It All Away

Everything we encounter in life is a deposit. Our wells are full of our life experiences and information. Giving it away brings hope to someone else. What are you leaving behind so the next generation will know you were here? All the gifts, talents and abilities the Creator so graciously gave us are for someone else. His hands move on our lives like an orchestra playing a symphony. The stage has been set and the curtains are drawn. The part He has designed you to play will keep the band flowing smoothly and in harmony. Each person is equipped with their own sound. Be willing to play your part.

It's very important for others to see and witness the good works He has placed in you. Deposit all that you are in the earth.

Each part is vitally connected to someone else. There are no pieces that do not need to be played. Others have deposited into our lives, be it a good experience or bad. We've learned from each. By giving it all out, the Creator will pour more in. He desires a channel, a vessel to move through. Don't look at yourself and question what you have to give. Look to Him and ask: "What do You want me to give?"

God has placed a treasure in every person to be located, activated, and then given all away. People need what we have just like we need what others have. It all fits together in God's scheme. Just be willing to play your part so others won't miss out on what God has for them.

I choose to die empty.

Choosing to Dream

"Our truest life is when we are in our dreams awake."
- Henry David Thoreau

"I will! I am! I can!
I will actualize my dream.
I will press ahead.
I will settle down and see it through.
I will solve the problems.
I will pay the price.
I will never walk away from my dream until I see the dream walk away: Alert! Alive! Achieved!"
- Robert Schuller

Chapter 12
Leaving a Legacy

Wanting to leave behind an aroma of a life once lived, I chose to follow the dream.

There is a connection one must have to dream. That connection comes from within. We connect with our Creator who holds the perfect design for our lives. When spending time in solitude, I ask specific questions. Intently listening, the answers come.

Dreams hold mysteries and secrets which are intended specifically for the dreamer. Our dreams need a safe landing place. In times of prayer and meditation, the heart is prepared to be the location.

Dreaming is a forward call, a forward motion. It has the ability to take you out of one situation and place you into your destiny. When the call is answered with a resounding yes, our Creator is in motion to set the stage for the journey. Connecting with the appropriate people at the right time, finding the book which holds the information that was needed or the promotion which causes more financial income is our Creators' way of assisting the dream. Choosing to dream will take your life further than you can ever imagine.

Choosing to dream is a spiritual commitment. It is an agreement between ourselves and God that we will do something towards investing in the future.

It takes strength and determination to follow your dream. Faith in God is essential. Belief in yourself is a critical principle which cannot be ignored. Having the ability to stand alone is a vital element in building a sturdy foundation.

You will have to fight for your dream. There will be some forms of resistance. The attack comes from taking a stand for what you believe. We have to be willing to go on dreaming and doing anyway.

Before I chose to dream, I lived a life from day to day with no hope or vision for the future. When I made a choice to believe the dream God placed in my heart, the vision began to take form.

Now I can see my destiny laid out before me like a picture painted on a canvas.

There are some hills.
There are some valleys.
There is thick green grass which looks as if it carpets the earth.
There are some majestic snow capped mountain peaks.
The sky is beautiful with a few storm clouds on the horizon.
But high above every hill, valley, meadow, mountain and cloud, the glory of the Son shines magnificent and bright, comforting me, strengthening me and leading me on.

It's never too late to dream.

My Future is a Matter of Choice

My future is a matter of choice
In obedience to God:
I choose to surrender my life to Him
I choose to live for Him wholly
I choose to serve Him for the rest of my days
I choose to trust God and Him only
I choose to walk and live by faith
I choose to live a life of worship and praise
I choose to live a life of hope
I choose to live a life of peace
I choose to live a life of joy
I choose to give what has been so freely given to me
I choose to love in all situations
I choose to live in victory
I choose to look to the hills from which comes my help
I choose to believe in the God in me
I choose to believe in myself
Therefore, my future is a matter of choice.

C. Lynn

Choosing to Dream
Chapter Affirmations

- **I choose to be an overcomer**
- **I choose to enjoy the ride**
- **I choose to laugh at myself**
- **I choose to trust in His work rather than my own**
- **I choose to love myself**
- **I choose to be willing to move**
- **I choose to take care of myself**
- **I choose to be content**
- **I choose to be only me**
- **I choose to do what it takes**
- **I choose to die empty**
- **It's never too late to dream**

Thank you so much for your purchase of:

Choosing to Dream

Please feel free to leave your comments by writing:

clynn@truevine.net

Don't forget to visit us at:

www.hatchbackpub.com

Choosing to Dream Order Form

Use this form to order:

Choosing to Dream

Please Print:
Name____
Address______________________________________
City____
State____
Zip Code_____________________________________
Phone (   )________________________________

__________**copies of book at $7.00 each** **$**__________
Postage & Handling @ $2.00 each **$**__________
Total Amount enclosed **$**__________

Make Checks Payable to:
HATCHBACK Publishing

Send to:
HATCHBACK Publishing
P.O. Box 480
Genesee, Michigan 48437

***Allow 3 to 5 weeks for delivery**